Praise for *Ancient Light*

"'Loss is a sentry, a watching,' writes Kimberly Blaeser in her latest collection of poems, *Ancient Light*. Emerging from the stillness and despair of a global pandemic, Blaeser's poems are elegiac, and they are wondrous elevations of a distinctly Anishinaabe world—a homescape in which humans and their stories are in kinship with the land. Blaeser's poems praise the legacies of 'antler earrings' and 'ruby star quilt[s]'; they follow the heron's arc of flight and the bounty of a tamarack woods. In a time most are lost, Blaeser's poems give us small rushes of direction like 'inky leaf shadows on snow.'"

—MOLLY MCGLENNEN, author of *Our Bearings*

"To read Blaeser's poems is to dive into a river and emerge transformed. Anyone who is learning to look with their whole being, anyone who has overcome, beat odds, endured—will be quenched by these waters. Beauty, tenderness, wisdom. All abide here in these 'language shapes, root-deep . . . with knowing.'"

—DANUSHA LAMÉRIS, author of *Bonfire Opera*

"Blaeser takes a step into what I've come to understand as the field of the page in this dazzling new work. The pages become water and the poems cause wave and ripple as if crane or heron. The poems 'swallow kinship' and move with the earth itself. *Ancient Light* is more than book: it's a map of a people thriving in a strange language or it's a manual with the sole purpose of show us how we arrive at 'our / sacred, / our / medicine.' As we endure crisis after crisis in a changing world, conquest induced, this book is the light, the sun through storm clouds, another radiant and hopeful morning."

—JAKE SKEETS, author of *Eyes Bottle Dark with a Mouthful of Flowers*

"*Ancient Light* is courageous and alive with the possibility of healing others through ceremony. Kimberly's poems are possessed of relentless syllabic innovation, hidden histories and flowing swaths of sun on grass. 'What is meter but another word for memory?' If we are in fact brave enough to begin our collective healing, let us open our hearts to this collection and listen closely. The silences are as chilling as the actual language. We are in the hands of a master. Such vividness is self-selecting."

—CEDAR SIGO, author of *Guard the Mysteries*

"Blaeser's poems transcribe the alchemical formula for turning memory to power, and power into being. Soft, lush strokes on a landscape of want and fullness, *Ancient Light* uncovers home with archaeological precision and an artist's keen eye. Kimberly Blaeser's work is what happens when a gifted poet uses their considerable tools to carve out specific belonging in an otherwise common existence, and we are all called to dream."

—CHERIE DIMALINE, author of *The Marrow Thieves*

Praise for Kimberly Blaeser

"These poems are small sure lights in the darkness—poems to lead us home. Kim Blaeser is exacting and precise. Her compassionate vision is the light."

—Joy Harjo, on *Absentee Indians*

"I turn . . . to Blaeser's many brilliant naturist efforts in the poetry here. . . . Her point is that the lives and languages of other species transcend human hubris. . . . Through . . . moments of uncanny epiphany . . . Blaeser's new collection of poems, *Apprenticed to Justice*, offers the reader a marvelous apprenticeship in itself. . . . The reader is 'apprenticed' into considerations of the possible erasure of our cognitive distinctions between vital life and 'dead' matter, between the animate and inanimate."

—Tom Gannon, *Prairie Schooner Review* of *Apprenticed to Justice*

ANCIENT LIGHT

Volume 94

Sun Tracks

An American Indian Literary Series

SERIES EDITOR

Ofelia Zepeda

EDITORIAL COMMITTEE
Larry Evers
Joy Harjo
Geary Hobson
N. Scott Momaday
Irvin Morris
Simon J. Ortiz
Craig Santos Perez
Kate Shanley
Leslie Marmon Silko
Luci Tapahonso

KIMBERLY BLAESER

Ancient Light

Poems

THE UNIVERSITY OF
ARIZONA PRESS
TUCSON

The University of Arizona Press
www.uapress.arizona.edu

We respectfully acknowledge the University of Arizona is on the land and territories of Indigenous peoples. Today, Arizona is home to twenty-two federally recognized tribes, with Tucson being home to the O'odham and the Yaqui. Committed to diversity and inclusion, the University strives to build sustainable relationships with sovereign Native Nations and Indigenous communities through education offerings, partnerships, and community service.

ISBN-13: 978-0-8165-5217-7 (paperback)
ISBN-13: 978-0-8165-5218-4 (ebook)

Cover design by Leigh McDonald
Cover art by Kimberly Blaeser
Designed and typeset by Leigh McDonald in Bell 10/14 and Canto Pen (display)

Publication of this book is made possible in part by support from The Virginia G. Piper Center for Creative Writing, and by the proceeds of a permanent endowment created with the assistance of a Challenge Grant from the National Endowment for the Humanities, a federal agency.

Library of Congress Cataloging-in-Publication Data
Names: Blaeser, Kimberly M., author.
Title: Ancient light : poems / Kimberly Blaeser.
Other titles: Sun tracks ; v. 94.
Description: Tucson : University of Arizona Press, 2024. | Series: Sun tracks : an American Indian literary series ; volume 94
Identifiers: LCCN 2023007047 (print) | LCCN 2023007048 (ebook) | ISBN 9780816552177 (paperback) | ISBN 9780816552184 (ebook)
Subjects: LCSH: Indians of North America—Poetry. | LCGFT: Poetry.
Classification: LCC PS3552.L3438 A85 2024 (print) | LCC PS3552.L3438 (ebook) | DDC 811/.54—dc23/eng/20230412
LC record available at https://lccn.loc.gov/2023007047
LC ebook record available at https://lccn.loc.gov/2023007048

Printed in the United States of America
♾ This paper meets the requirements of ANSI/NISO Z39.48-1992 (Permanence of Paper).

In memory of those lost to the pandemic and the centuries-long plague of violence.
May our communities heal.
To relatives (blood and soul)—gratitude. *Gizhawenimin.*

CONTENTS

III.

IV.

ANCIENT LIGHT

Akawe, a prelude

i.

Between languages—in the shadow of old losses, we adorn ourselves.

ii.

Words join breath marks, fall into silence. Language stutters and searches—
an odyssey. Etched in bark eyes, in patterns on rock, in absence.

Everywhere, careful words break—open, they feed us. Remembrance like bread.

iii.

An arithmetic of spirals. In this reckoning, seasons repeat their chorus. Chant
noodin, nibi, ishkode, aki. This way we swallow kinship.

iv.

How song names the shattered, shifts gravity. Call it map, duende, or *zaagi'idiwin.*

Language filaments ephemeral—in motion, they become transparent.

v.

Wave patterns. Cloud warnings. Animal musk. Insects from nymph to imago;
plants, bud to harvest to seed. Night howls, crane calls, discordant yip of coyote.

Our dwelling a literacy. A blessing we inhabit.

Here we grieve, honor, and sometimes devour.

vi.

Now from our tongues a salve—an animal saliva called language.

Mikwendaman—retelling we wake, seek repair.

vii.

Tethered to moon by ritual, desire. *Apane*—this way, we continue.

i

Poem on Disappearance

Beginning with our continent, draw 1491:
each mountain, compass-point Indigenous;
trace trade routes, languages, seasonal migrations—
don't become attached.
Yes, reshape by discovery,   displacement,
move your pencil point quickly now as if pursued—
a cavalry of possession that erases
homelands: we shrink shrink—in time-lapse
of colonial barter . . . disappear   .

Now draw a brown face painted for ceremony,
half a face, nothing

     .

Draw nothing around a crumbled bird body—
no wings.

Draw emptiness inside desecrated burial mounds,
a stretch of absence where fallopian tubes once curved in hope,
sketch void across buffalo prairie, draw the empty
of elk, of passenger pigeons, of silver trout.

Conjure with your hand the shape of girl
blooming, curves of face, her laughing eyes;
you've seen them postered and amber-alerted—
missing, missing, evening newsed, and gone.

Draw a woman wrapped in a blanket,
a child's body weighted—draw stones
sinking into every river on the map.

Draw carrion blackening skies, carrion
plucking vision from round brown faces—
draw missing, draw murdered.

Work carefully now,
turn your hand to the new continent.
Again picture it—

                    nothing   .

Truce

The *brush-catch-brush-catch* rhythm of days,
her pulling pink bristles through tangles,
feeding my hair into and out of ponytail holders.
I brace each time for the small pain,
the extra tightness, the tug at my roots:
how the missing fingers on her hand
make of this rote task—of us—a stutter.
(The specter of boarding school never leaves—
an accident, an old injury scarred over.)
My silent promise not to flinch,
her huff of breath like squelched anger.
Neither wants to show the slippery trying—
how we two must entwine to balance
on one dark tendril   of loss.

Plead the Blood

Now search for stories they have buried
like bodies—

        silence of hidden graves.

How we unearth night-crawler truths:

children   and words (they whispered

        cot   to   cot)

           where dark rituals

found them—   devoured.

Oh, holy edifice where robe-blessed led,
schooled in terror   brown charges,

how claim the
           unnamed
                from Wiindigoo

territories.   Bargain in language of tabernacle

for sifted earth   remnants,

                          lost futures.

Our stolen—restolen.

Taxonomy

The ancestors live in boxes now. I live squared—
only head. The world is blue screen, is scream.
Name something intact—without acronyms.

Morning cormorant a silhouette—elongated
in familiar, a routine of hunger then bulk.
We swallow whole the impossible. No one
feeds prettily. Avert your eyes, survive.

The ancestors live in white—cardboard boxes.
I am fasting. No news feed. Or rumor. Politics
a super spreader. How we shelter in non-places.

Here the hooked bill of the cormorant fills
(I ignore the chat, have exited the zoom room).
My dry throat opens—to swallow, convulses
by reflex or instinct. Waterbirds, we live this story.

Ancestors wait on shelves in numbered boxes.

They dive, propel themselves with webbed feet.
Shaggy cormorant wings spread wide to dry.
Perhaps we are not praying when we lift our hands.

Xtracted like resources

SQUAW

Rewritten in caricature as history's princess whore.

Vanishment
↓

WhoRWe?.

bodies Woman a99 keening
Each dark strand
See us
?
now
Istanding upons no9
strong limbed out bodies
MMIW
BUR story shadows
I E S
b o D i e s
WeWeWe branches
Who rise
from erasure
Remember us
Follow like shadows
each disappearance
XX X X X X X X X X X
each gone ikwewag —
Bled or buried. We remain
Mortgaged morality of America return
This haunting along outwaiting

Here rooted tribal like trees goldest belonging

Drowned.
Discarded.
Dishonored.

Howwee

forged

Reckoning

AXXXE

S_ CR_D

see us sacred ≠ Xtracted

(a transcript)

Caricature
swings in history

✝ beam
bears weight of red:

                                        pendulum—

                   ~~princess~~   w   whore
                                         h
                      ~~princess~~   o   whore
                                         R
                        ~~princess~~   w   whore
                                         e
                                         ?

A body ⌈SQUAW⌉—
red-ribbed chest—
hold of the hyphenated
(read BURIED).

X X X X (a decorative line) X X X
each gone ikwewag (   ).

Bled or buried. We
remain remains.
Invisible as stench—

This skirt edge of haunting
scarlets a long outwaiting.

Object of game,
crude stick-figure,
we call her:

                      Refuses-the-Rope.

Anti-Sonnet on Rivers

These patched-together college afternoons—
a deli counter, a book with bent pages,
cannot soothe nor mend your ravaged knuckles,
retrieve *savage* bones grave-stolen and bartered
nor unwrap bound bodies of drowned sisters.
That diary that declares us *ingenious*
also predicts our future, paper damns us
with thin praise or colonial gaze:
ink-spells how we *would be good servants*,
would very readily become Christians.
Carelessly words transfigure us, mutate
in American mascot fashion our fate.
Today our redskin blackhawk wrath spills
into crimson rivers—ancient and rising.

English Lessons

My Mother Learns to Spell

In the reservation school
my mother had a trick for remembering
the frail English letters of spelling words:
she released them like too-small fish

$\qquad\qquad\qquad$ *giigoozensag*

into the landscape, imagined them in motion.
She chanted each chalk mark   alive—

$\qquad\qquad\qquad$ swimming away.

> $\qquad$ *M-I-*
> $\qquad$ *crooked letter*
> $\qquad\quad$ *crooked letter*
> $\qquad\qquad$ *(the name*
> $\qquad\qquad\quad$ *a picture—*
> $\qquad\qquad\qquad$ *meandering,*
> $\qquad\qquad$ *snaking river beds*
> $\qquad$ *the **ssss** of flow)*
> $\qquad\qquad$ *I*
> $\qquad$ *crooked letter*
> $\qquad\quad$ *crooked letter*
> $\qquad\qquad$ *I*
> $\qquad\qquad\quad$ *P*
> $\qquad\quad$ *P*
> $\qquad\qquad$ *I*

Gichi-ziibi

15

ii.
Another Lesson in Orthography

When Winona spells it   P-O-W-E-R

is an expletive   (like fracking).

    Progress advance future innovation—

each synonym for *take* a clearcutting.

Sharp-edged language of Industry—an axe
                to cedar
                to birch
                to white-pine belonging.

Cutting pipeline passages
                to extinction.

iii.
(In the lodge)

Fossil fuels are the remains
of living organisms.

    Leave them buried.

Like relatives.

In the pause before you speak

you will wonder who brought crimson,
who dared scarlet the white place setting.

I am not saying I sent my doppelganger
—not saying, but you will wonder.

At your toast, more than one eye will dart—
the room will fill, cool with uninvited.

You will want the applause to sound different,
less like red hands red dresses red hollow.

You will wonder what went wrong in America—
this real estate you call your country.

I am not saying the fabric is unraveling,
pulling apart where your voice has snagged.

But you will hear mumbles about fires and climate—
your eyes will burn in the silence of who to blame.

When we have lost enough

At the juncture of "enough,"
loss becomes a river, a power-
ful undertow, a torrent sometimes,
but a current on which we travel.

Loss is a sentry, a watching
& always the motion of eyes—
their cartoon arrows of glare,
your brown iris black pupil
seeing themselves in water,
leaving themselves—vacant
vacated, those eyes in water
watching themselves pass.

I have seen crocodiles in Africa
floating like a ripple or wake,
camouflaged except for the globe
of watching, their eyes a bubble
surfacing like drowned fears,
a lurk, a stare, a stalk—a follow.

I have seen snapping turtles
big as a baby's bathtub,
barely submerged, barely
visible apparition of silt
swimming, their bulbous
eyes ancient—patient as death.

To that book-sharp gaze—
the one we call colonial,
we have lost enough.
Cold. Like an ox-eye
warning of storm.
Always fixed on me. On you.
We pursued measured
appraised like a crumbling nation
put up for quick sale—reduced.

When we have lost,
when we have lost enough,
we lift our white-schooled tired—
lift loss like a sail.
We have not drowned, not
been swallowed by empire.
We steely, eyes forward,
hoist our starquilt sorrow—
half-mast & learn to steer.

Dead Letter

i.

Kneeling before what god
on another man's neck?

How we lynch now

in America—a forgery
of justice. *Protect and Serve*
defunct as dead letter laws.

George Floyd another notch
on the pearl handle of power.

Tamir Rice. Breonna Taylor.
Eric Garner. Dontre Hamilton.
notch. notch. power notch.

(Spell me another word for master.)

Picture postcards of lynching—
sent √.

Videos of murder by police—
addressed to each hall of justice:

undeliverable—addressee unknown.

ii.

"& what if hope crashes through the door"*

Migizi burns, a riot of flames, a sorrow—
of suffocating bodies. *I can't breath*

your toxic, America. Sell me windpipe
dreams—of cedar fluted breath, a song

for continuing. For continuing in our shelter
in our streets, without the phallic generals.

For continuing beyond slave ships and war
ships and Nina-Pinta-and-Santa-Maria ships.
Beyond chains, treaties, internment camps,
boarding schools and segregated schools,
removals and reservations, the phrenology
of race and race and race . . .

How we race now, America—

to new emancipation: NO PEACE
WITHOUT JUSTICE. Let us mask
ourselves in hope—all broken of these histories.

Kneel now together and count—
Nine minutes to change.

* From "Elegy" by Mong-Lan.

On the Dignity of Gestures

for Nathan Phillips

i.

Remember hands, ungloved and notched by life. Watch them pour stove-top
coffee into tin cups, lift cross poles onto fence bucks, mend nets, rock your children.

ii.

Pay homage and speak the names of sweepers and shovelers, canners, cafeteria
cooks, baby doctors, and death-bed watchers. Esme, Dale, Margaret, David, Mike,
and Colleen.

iii.

Receive all gifts (crocheted afghan or prize money) with humility. Gratitude
spreads easy as butter; unworthiness endures.

iv.

Watch the eyes of turtle. Admire the neck-courting of swans. Study wingbeats
and tail rhythms. Note how otter sows stoop to lift pups. Listen to wind in fall,
to trees bending and unbroken. Announce like spring frogs the unfolding of each
holy year. Carry candles into cathedrals, poetry into prisons.

v.

Do not become beast in the fray. Remember the Indigenous hands that drummed
on, the man who stood calm.

An allegory in which there are politicians and false promises

We need to stage earnest satirical plays,
hold debate contests with farm animals
at midnight.
—Ishmael Hope

Even now reimagine the animals into nativity—
a wholesome fantasy where they merely low before saviors,
where we are simple shepherds awed by lights in the sky.

Haven't we always followed shine?

How we love the flickering aurora and the steady
curve of rainbow—who doesn't wonder at the glistening
in all its crayola promise?

Yes, once there was a star. A midnight turning.

But come up from your knees.

Tonight put on old albums. Let the scratchy vinyl
soothe our hunger. Touch the intricate quillwork
of *makakoon*—baskets ageless with sweetgrass rims.
Again unlock secret red diaries and open
dog-eared pages. Once there were stories by fires,
blessings sung in cedar smoke circles.

Can we be animals who dress in our history?
Remake its moldy sweet armor:
a shield, shelter, a coat of mail—or ransom
from tweet wars and evening news—an answer
to false promises like election and salvation.

december 2019

feeding myself on winter light
even in the dark days of trump

how we survive now spooling
sky—tendrils of softest morning

our muted blue days woven
with weft of tawny slivers

pale wash of hope pulled close
encircles us like silk scarves

warms our longing with horizon
an arc of amber—this small civility

About Standing (in Kinship)

We all have the same little bones in our foot,
twenty-six with funny names like *navicular*.
Together they build something strong—
our foot arch a pyramid holding us up.
These bones don't get casts when they break.
We tape them—one *phalange* to its neighbor for support.
(Other things like sorrow work that way, too—
find healing in the leaning, the closeness.)
Our feet have one quarter of all the bones in our body.
Maybe we should give more honor to feet
and to all those tiny but blessed cogs in the world—
communities, the forgotten architecture of friendship.

The Way We Love Something Small

In deepest winter. *Here,*
when I turn from rebuttal.

Ice gathers   *crackle*
sings under snow boots
                        shatters
and reforms.

Hoarfrost feathers adorn each surface
white on white—
my eyes confess
a longing for oldest patterns
aki, earth's intricate
a writ consolation.

Each frozen word
            on lips of water
a sweet note—

        a mended silence.

Here We Begin With Gesture

Bill bends—his left leg a stiffening
he works around. On three we lift
one fallen cross pole, then another.
With red bandana he mops his brow.

Twelve feet away a tv crew itches—
counting down. Their deadline is news feed.

This repair is not the work, but the preamble.
White pine. Wooden grave houses.
Fragrant grains of kinnikinnick dampen
as we hold them (in the left, the heart hand).

Nearby ferns and grasses sway like dancers,
their songs steady (not gone)—a soft *shu-shu*
while Ninzhishenh's rimy bird voice rises,
Our tobacco gift, our words, placed—just so.

Suddenly Uncle straightens, lengthens his neck
to stare through dark Buddy Holly IHS rims,
fixes on the expectant lens of the KSTP camera—
tripod and glass viewfinder squaring our world.

Now his chin lifts, his lips, his flannelled arm;
they arc slowly like the sun cupping the land—
giizis carressing Anishinaabe-akiing dawn to dusk.
All of us wait. In the silence of old trees, still standing.

The Way We Love Something Small

Vowel sounds from a land
language not yet lost:
Mooningwanekaaning-minis.
My tongue an island, too,
swimming   where *Migis* rises.
This ache tiny but growing—

the place I keep it.

ii

The Where in My Belly

Scientists say my brain and heart
are 73 percent water—
they underestimate me.

A small island—*minis*, I emerged
among Minnesota's northern lakes,
the where of *manoomin*—wild rice in my belly.

I am from boats and canoes and kayaks,
from tribal ghosts who rise at dawn
dance like wisps of fog on water.

My where is White Earth Nation
and white pine forests,
knees summer-stained with blueberries,
pink lady slippers open and wild as my feet.

I grew up where math was canasta,
where we recited times tables
while ice fishing at twenty-below,
spent nights whistling to Northern Lights.

I am from old: medicines barks and teas;
from early—the air damp with cedar
the crack of *amik*, beaver tails on water.

Their echo now a warning to where—
to where fish become a percentage of mercury,
become a poison statistic;
to where copper mines back against
a million blue acres of sacred.

I am from *nibi* and *ogichidaakweg*,
women warriors and water protectors, from seed-
gatherers and song-makers,

the wet where pulse in my belly whispers and repeats
like the endless chant of waves on ledgerock,
waves on ledgerock   on ledgerock   on waves

                                        on water . . . *nibi.*

Dipped with cupped hands

slowly
to remember the taste.

Creek cold
funnels like story
all similar moments:

sharp-tongued melt of icicles
rock flavor of camp streams
mouth on mitten of snow crystals
green scent of lake tea.

What the sieve of our bodies holds:

sweet sap drip in spring
wet wood—the linger.

This hint of land's red—
iron ore,
our history.

Oh Sisters
 of dark earth
      r
       o
        o
         t
          e
           d

            H E R E.

Nookwezigan—our medicine plants

Gitigaanan

Oh Sisters
       of dark earth
           r
              o
                o
                  t
                    e
                  d

           H E R E.

Where   tribal lands hold us   we flower

    seasons on end   go   to   seed.

Oh floral and feral!

Ikwewag and *nookwezigan*—our women ash spreading like freedom,

                 our medicine plants:

chokecherry tobacco cedar sage sweetgrass diamond willow
wild mint skunk cabbage elderberry cattails balsam bloodroot
plantain yarrow jo-pye arrow root panic grass tamarack bulrush.

Praise the uncultivated meadows of our bodies,

        dream now of coppering like leaves—

            fallow and holy of time.

Understory

Jiisens
 a taproot
in glacial soils,
   this medicine relative—
kin to Anishinaabeg.

Gikinawaabi—
(we learn by watching)
 Oh, ginseng
   in your dark waiting,
 you teach us
    patience.

We count sacred numbers:
 leaves and stem scars—
    our markers
(old stories, too, tell the buried)
 four years to flowering,
   ten to harvest.

How *Midewiwin* healers see
   red berries—
      a promise.

Songs Like Bread: *Wiikwandiwin*

Inhabited, we whisper and sort
tongue hungers,

this blood caress of gone
an almost melody;

nooji'ikwewe-nagamon
courting song (how we yearn)

for morsels, words—memory-tangle
of hands (k)neading *bakwezhigan*—

this dollop of sweetest dough
a language prisoner's bread.

This is to hunger (*bakade)*
this is to break (*biigoshkaad),*

to speak is to eat
wiikwandiwin, feast food

our jagged stuttering a giveaway—
maada'oonidiwag (this is to share).

Found Recipe, *Mikinaak Dibaajimowin*

i.

A tiny woman who'd slept with hunger, my grandma dreamed always of warm food. Wild rice flavored with berries and venison fat. Fresh fish, coated and cooked on an open fire. Turtle soup, above all else.

Even into old age, Nookomis could never resist any food that wandered across her path. Always with a bag for gathering nuts, a sharp pocketknife for wild asparagus, she padded along, kerchiefed and bent like a letter C.

Poor snapper. *Mikinaak.* Who would have expected it? He grabbed the long oak branch, hung on just as she said he would.

His shell already a rattle in her brown hands.

ii.

You cut the turtle into pieces, she instructs. (Never ask how you extract it from the shell.) *Brown it in the oven uncovered. Keep the heat at 400 to 425.*

Carrying wood is the easy part. She lets me do this. Meanwhile she is humming under her breath as she collects things: a crock from the cloth-covered cupboards, root vegetables from the damp earth of the cellar. *For extra flavor, add some veal knuckles.* She sighs at this. *Trade something, it will be worth it.*

What does one trade for veal knuckles?

I start to ask, but she has moved on to *tender green onions. Mushrooms in cream—pour that over the turtle. Salt and pepper. Paprika.* My grandma was always one for paprika. I thought it odd, to measure from the tin, when other herbs came fresh, tied in bundles, or sometimes right from her apron.

Let the fire go down a bit now, my girl. 325. 350. I peer in the little glass door at the logs turning to ash. Try to gauge degrees from the sweat that trickles on my brow. *The turtle don't mind,* she laughs. I think she means the extra heat. Means the recipe isn't particular.

But then I see her pat the vacant shell. *Nope, it don't mind.*

iii.

We clean up while wood crackles softly, like a voice making a promise. Nakoomis makes no easy promises. *It takes some time. Dibaajimowin. We wait until it's tender.* Tender story?

We still have time. Always had more time than money.

My stomach is rumbling now and I want to ask how long. But I'm suddenly uncertain—is this still turtle talk? With the old ones you never know. Some following has no recipe. That *mikinaak* on my Grandma's stick. Me on the braid end of her quick hands.

Naboobiins, she says. *This little soup. Three to four hours.*

 Story soup. Tender meat. Just as I latch on, she's off again. *Depends upon the size. And age, of course.* She gives me a nudge now with the broom. *Young is better.* She laughs then and repeats herself. *Young is better. But when you're hungry, old will do.*

I hear sap pop in the cook-fire, like a turtle rattle, like the tobacco break in my Grandma's laugh.

iv.

My job is to watch. Every twenty minutes or so I poke the little chunks swimming in the savory sauce. My grandma has fallen asleep, the scent of dinner working like a lullaby.

I imagine she still dreams of old hungers. And odd moments of fullness.

The meal we wait for. The making of it.

Of Universal Suffrage

26,000,000 american women
sashed and marched into history.
500 ancient nations—marginal notes
in the sweet anthem of equality.
Indigenous non-citizens—still.

Women *holding our world together*
in the dusky and lawless violence
manifest in colonial america.

In the trombone slide of history
I hear the *suffer* in *suffragette:*
    [In late middle English
    intercessory prayers,
    a series of petitions.
    Not the right—but the hope.]
the *uni uni uni* in *universal:*
    [*Applicable to all cases*—
    except those marginalized
    and unnamed.
    A belief, but not a fact.]

Each excluded ikwe. Nookomisag:
mindimooyenh or matriarchs.
Turn to the older congress of the sun,
seek in the assembled stories of sky
a steady enlightenment—natural laws
(sistering of nutrients—maizebeanssquash,
the mathematics of bending trees
or wintering wisdom of animal relatives)
each seasonal chorus colored with resilience—
earth voices rising in sacred dream songs.

Even now listen, put on the moon-scored
shell of turtle, wear this ancient armor

of belonging. In the spiral of survivance
again harvest the sweet maple sap of trees,
follow the scattered path of manoomin,
the *wild and good seed* that grows on water.

Oh water, oh rice, oh women of birch dreams
and baskets, gather. Here harvest and reseed,
raise brown hands trembling holy with endurance.
Now bead land-knowledge into mukluks,
sign with the treaty X of exclusion.
Kiss with fingers and lips the inherited
woodland flutes and breathy cedar songs.
Say yea, eya, and yes. Here and here cast
your tended nets—oh suffered and sweetly mended
nets of abundance. This year and each to follow,
choose not by paper but by pathway, a legacy
of *woman's work*, our ancient ballad of continuance.

A Water Poem for Remembering

Yes, it's true I speak ill of the living
in coded ways divorced from the dead.
Why Lyla June fasts on capitol steps.
Why Native women disappear like rabbits,
reappear in rivers wrapped in death scarves.
A leader's slight of voice a disgrace—
we've been magicked before into war.
Why we sing *mikwendam*—even now
remember. On the coldest day of January
gather near ancestral waters, *Michigami*
(where the Milwaukee, Menominee,
& Kinnickinnic rivers meet like sisters)
where conical mounds still rise on bluffs,
story *good pathways*—bold and blue as *nibi.*

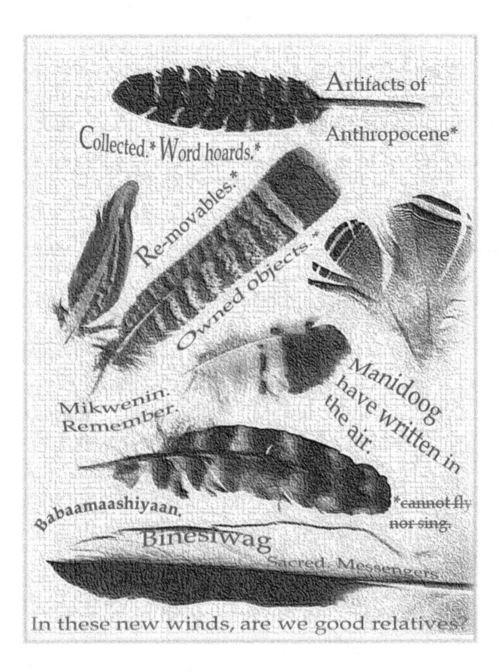

Artifacts of

Anthropocene*

Collected.* Word hoards.*

Re-movables.*

Owned objects.*

Mikwenin.
Remember.

Manidoog
have written in
the air.

Babaamaashiyaan.

*cannot fly
nor sing.

Binesiwag

Sacred. Messengers.

In these new winds, are we good relatives?

Binesiwag

The Way We Love Something Small

In the wake of bare
we like trees—waiting.

Even now sap runs in maple—
from snow, spring and crocus;
from bloom, a solace.
Each day, each blossom purples

                with ritual.

Wash in the chorus of spring peepers
in the startle of crane calls:
each oldest song

                survivance.

Rosetta stone

or fractals of moose antlers

velveted in spring,
rising   into copper sky—
ishpiming.

The water-winged
unreality of delicately scored
and mottled lily pads,

olive and crimson mandalas—
a scatter graph   across
the impossible,   the blue.

These discs of foliage,
tessellations of bone.

Their submerged rhizomes—
ours,   how they tattoo us
with the script
                    of place,

with language shapes
root-deep—
          with knowing.

These Ways We Practice *Mino-bimaadiziwin*

Beneath deepest summer skies we swim
among Anishinaabeg stars stories, now sing

                                to night wanderers.

We tame the two-thin needles that hunger,
thread them lavishly with colored seed beads—

                                counting and layering.

Here, too, we study the palest sketches of beauty:
trace each toe of animal tracks, touch water marks

                                on ancient ledge rock,

watch pollen color June lakes golden, then sepia,
whisper to each helicopter seed pod that lifts

                                on Minnesota winds.

This *good path* becomes a tune we hum beneath days
steady as the chest's drumbeat, clear as that oldest language—

                                apane, of belonging.

The Language of Sphere

Kawishiwi. A circle of latitude 48° north. Where small chips fly out from the furious beak of a pileated.

We are late in crossing and hunger pushes us. All around the inferno of autumn blazes, fills even the water with copper. With redbronzelemongold and brightest orange—with swallowed glory.

Even as we feast then on the color, winds of decay resist our paddling, and the baring of branches continues. This honeyed air—the last exhale of leaves.

Woodpeckers, too, like fire in the trees. *Plunk, plunk. Plunk,* then *tick.* The head blur unearthing dinner, bark's cache of larvae.

We are in this somewhere.

As leaves, perhaps. Or only their refractions—a rippled image on river. Say we are the roots tapping groundwater, the branches drinking. Or are we the manic head, the endless motion searching survival? Who would claim the beetle for clan? Hard-shelled and burrowing further into darkness. Who eats tree, who kills it.

But watch these layers. Hunger and fullness—too deep for measure.

The skin of the tree broken, open. Insects lifted from winding tunnels. The bark now a calligraphy of holes. Hollowed, but not empty. Shall I tell you nature knows no vacuum—only cycle?

How soon the red squirrel. How soon each tongue hunts. How deep the sap.

Yes—the sweetness.

The Way We Love Something Small

A wetland filled with white—
egret heronry. Oh mythic wings
and plumes of spring!

Watch now the sleek-feathered stalk:

each patient long-legged   lift
    and step
        of black branch legs.

The uncurving—

as S of neck lengthens
   points the green-masked dagger eye
the hungry skewer beak.

Suspended here on the brink:
the stillness before motion.

Only me naming it—
my head counting   second   by hushed   second
    finally   forgetting
numbers   and   all   the words

for grace.

A Catalogue of Migration

Here in the dictionary of sky
dagwaagin may mean full,
mean cobalt holding motion of wings,
wings bending clock, bending time, again.
Endaso dagwaagin—every fall: breath,
eternity blowing cycle—watch air streams funnel
then unfurl like rivers, swirl and sing—
nagamon this pouring of bird bodies.

Beneath departing talons and tail feathers
amid the trumpeting call of *waabizii,*
mighty wingspan of owl—*gookooko'oo,*
everywhere mallard, oriole, checker-backed loons,
soon air fills with echo of sandhill crane calls—
fluted and eternal like *doodem* dreamsongs.
Where every flap follows ancient flight paths,
bineshiinyag mark autumn sky, mark me.

Fall-lean, the trees become tipi poles
circled in migration, hold up the tent of sky.
Here in a dome of belonging where each wet
alive touches another god body, touches being,
noodin blows, pine tips bow low like suitors—
here beneath this lush, this blessed orgy.

Mashkiki, This Medicine Earth

Here a landscape endures—a vestige of before;
beyond mask, abundance for ailing human souls.
Oh sweet glimmer—white frost a sprinkle on winter prairie,
marshland a glazed and ghostly paradise where ice crackles
echo and echo across the expanse of its mirrored floor.
Here we small, we holy disappear into etched ice patterns;
swallowed by reflection, we trace belonging skin to skin.
Like land inscribed, we harbor stories, walk each ancient pathway
where tribal mounds still rise, hallowed and endless as copper memory.
In this curved alcove of sandy shoreline, waterfowl dive and feed and bob.
We pledge allegiance to the water—*nibi* relations wet and blessed.
Here a rock point stretches black into winter water,
this outcropping a gesture, an arrow we follow.
Then *abracadabra*! Each round rock suddenly plump and feathered,
a gathering of dark knowledge rising.
Oh, shelf of duck
launching into air!
Like the sigh
from my lips—
the song.
Praise the peninsula of
human body.
We surrounded
by gifts of water
breathing plants
this healing earth:
Aki,
our
sacred,
our
medicine—
m
a
s
h
k
i
k
i.

iii

Alaskan poems you didn't write

live like drum beats under your skin—
whisper scratch you on the other side of sound.
What is meter but another word for memory?

> *caribou bending to water in blue light,*
> *the unreality of mountain peaks at dawn,*
> *endless tundra littered with shed antlers—*

all jagged and boned glimpses of eternity.

We watch days bump suns in Alaskan skies
our pockets empty of words for measure:
how eloquent this lapping—
                              against singularity.

Dream of birch-winged eagles

Sandhill Sky

                    above us
each   body   a   crossed   t t t   t
      oh, flock

indoodem
                       f o r m i n g and   r e   f o r m i n g
          sky w r i t i n g
                   with   wings
    and stick-straight crane legs trailing
                out behind and behind lengthening beyond belief
no,
we are not trained to read sky
               but our resistance   yields
  to throaty   r o l l of song
                 the ancient   filling day and   echoing
        a sonorous chorus
            encircles us
        we wrapped in sound—enraptured
          ah
        the s w o o p of cranes, the s i e g e
          their motion
a choreography s p e l l i n g and re-spelling
                membe r ing   an alphabet
a pause   before   text

ajijaakwag
           a vision   airy   and sweet
    a blue harmonics
this ether
    essence of
         emptiness   now filled

my journal records the vestiture of doppelgangers

i.

Remember how the loon chick climbs to the mother's back.
Oh, checkerboard bed and lifted wing—oh, tiny gray passenger
who settles: eyes drooping closed, webbed foot lifted like a flag!
Each day, each week, I write missives—*Mayflies' transparent wings*
a stained glass—fluttering across the surface of lake. An impermanence.
Imagos who transform: molt mate glitter as splayed bodies on water.
I write *the red crown, mad V of vulture—wings drying in morning sun.*
I record *red squirrel swimming (yes! swimming) across a small channel.*

ii.

I barely breathe watching the narrow body (a mere slit of motion)
dark and steady like all mysterious—*paddle, paddle,* and *arrive*
now climb bedraggled and spent onto the small safety of a floating log.
It rests. We catch our breath. Now it scurries ahead to the other log end.
Here my journal stutters with a squirrel story bigger than words:
Unfathomably, it plunges back into blue chance—into uncharted.
We are never done, it says, with a body tiny enough to know.
The world is large, it says, with a courage I am greedy to learn.

iii.

Praise here all fabulous unwritten. Each shimmer of spent body,
journey from rest to blue next. Who, I ask, is the blissful beaver
devouring each yellow water lily if not our doppelganger?
Continually, I feel paws pulling, mouth filled with flower lust—
what little rooms are words in these seasons of plenty.

The Way We Love Something Small

In the cold blur hour of winter
the world wound tight and blue,
while we fold and triangle white paper.
Our kindergarten scissors an act of god—
we open close and fractal, replicating.

Even then our tenderness too big
                    for accuracy.

The Way We Love Something Small

Window open to Mahnomen night
a damp eternity   vibrating.

Alone.

Waking
to train whistle over a prairie town.

Bare feet pad
                  pum pum   through the dark house
each creak familiar as my father's face.

A dreamwalker moving by instinct.

Minnesota hands unlatch the screen door
cornstalks sway with *whisper* and *shush*
while the rabbit in the clover stills
his whiskers the second hand twitching
endlessly ticking
like the teapot clock saying

                        time
                            time
                                time
                                    time
into my bones.

Engine boxcar freight hopper hopper . . . caboose—
                        two blocks away in dewy dark.

Blue on Blue

In his favorite blue sweater,
in slippers and gloveless.
There in the Minnesota winter
paused in his backyard—
hand on the sleeping lilac.
A half-smile for me,
the photographer who sees
what in that moment?
One of his many fedoras
tipped at a precise angle?
Like the earth in each season
dancing with the distant sun:
lonely the tilt of time,
lilt of his song—rising?
Because he wears blue on blue,
because the light says evening
at his back. Because always
without jacket, empty-handed—
nor bulge of keys in his pocket.
Because the snow at his feet
seeps in, cold and marked
with tracks—rabbits and birds.
Because his knees, too, poise to lift
and step. On his way where
in that frame, in this?
Because I lean in to azure past—
leave this camera eye behind.

The Knife My Father Gave Me at Eight

One inch longer than my empty ring finger,
no field-master multi-function wonder,
a single blade Case slimline trapper
pocketknife my brother would teach me
to thumb—*open closed open closed open* again
until I could slide it out quick and smooth,
until I could point it, flick my wrist
throw and sink it every time blade first
in the sweet summer White Earth clay,
respect it, wipe it clean on my jeans.
The knife my father gave me at eight
whispered to me the things he left unsaid.
Small, sharp, and pearl-handled pretty—
it does the work of any man's blade.

Indian Baby in Front of an Indian Bldg., Albuquerque, NM

There, kerchiefed and content
in your lava soapbox throne,
you sit like a little turtle
in the familiar sun.

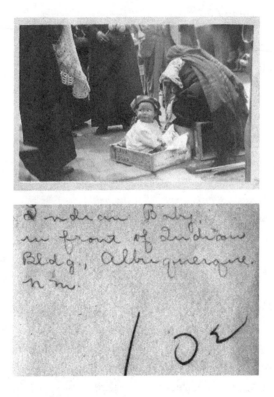

You, *Indian Baby in Front of an Indian Bldg.,*
photographed & captioned—
collected.

Saucer-eyed,
amid the airy swag of crocheted shawl,
behind you on crate seat
there, too, the comforting waterfall

of a fringed headscarf.

The soft crepe of your gown
folding like flesh
as in your Buddha sit
you gather a child's measure.

> *Hello melon plump arms.*
> *Aaniin little gourd wrists.*

Just there, Buddha child,
circle of woven bracelet
indents the putty of your flesh.

You tattooed
adorned as these women
by a mark of tribe or clan.

> *Hello, orphaned snapshot moments*
> *Hello, claymation*
> *Clipped from reality like bargain coupons*

Me, blonde Indian baby in the laundry basket,
Me, berry-plump and moon-eyed,
purse-mouthed amid Anishinaabe grandmothers.
Fishing women who tended me—
kwe of ceremonial fires and overturned buckets,
their simple radiance
spilling like a scarecrow's stuffing.

> Bartered photos, swap meet remnants,
> lost and tattered postcards—
> *Buy one get one!*

But boozhoo, survival.
Boozhoo tended embers of ancient light—
fire in the flint of a child's eye.

Some Math Formula

i.

Crooked and crane-thin, my uncle's legs
remember—polio, childhood injuries,
sometimes buckle under him.
I understand his surprise.

My hands lift kings, queens,
and jacks into walls, careful
this house with an ace for a roof—
my card castles felled by a dog's tail.

Uncle's flannel laugh and spindly legs fold—
both bend like an extension ladder;
brown thumbs shuffle my flattened kingdoms,
we cut, re-deal—bet matchsticks like we mean it.

ii.

I watch the unreal hinge on herons
how their knobby kneecaps flex, necks
twist, supporting cartoon head-dives for fish—
I rewrite some math formula in my head.

Perhaps heaviness or flight is an arc we trace
with the pencil of belief as much as with bodies,
perhaps necessity numbs pain, and the crack
from my uncle's knees may be lightning.

We go blueberry picking in tamarack woods
and my pail fills slowly slowly between bites,
plunk plunk, like his stuttering step, *plunk plunk*—
as the ripe weight of his berries multiplies mine.

The Way We Love Something Small

Sun through lace spills   delicate
shadow
          and wall remembers hands
remembers me   a child watching
crochet needles   *click, click*   like analog.

When I tire of explaining—

time a warm and tended fire
a compass   wheelbarrow   a flour-sifter
cream can   winnowing basket—

a tune we hum
                    wordless as sun, as lace, as shadow.

How Love Balances on Each Precipice

How she stood of a morning at the clothesline,
hummed, her song filled with dew-scented grass,
held the wooden clothespins in bruised lips.
How she lifted, then shook out the lilac sheets,
waved them, slapped the air with a loud crack—
how she never once flinched at the sound.

Him sitting, shoulders sunken, on the side of a bed
bent beneath the weight of words flung like fists.
His wrinkled arms nearly white as his undershirt,
large-knuckled hands like quiet birds in his lap.
How they open and lift—the flight of failed gesture,
a question that circles—the chorus of song.

Days I measured intentions, blood, and letters sent;
how in turns I loved each of them—more than the other.

This Small Curtained Space

Why write the bar scenes
the waiting in Minnesota winter car scenes,
if you have survived them?
Yet who will it hurt now
when the only breathing souls left
are the ones who watched the pool cues,
the bottles, fists, cigarettes, kisses,
the weeping and bleeding? Long ago
we sold the closets, the shower,
the small curtained space under the sink—
all the places that also held our silences.
Why now when the memories
have outlived everything except the walk-up music,
songs that played endlessly in the background—
those lyrics of love and betrayal
still spin on the small turntable,
the needle stuck and repeating:
Your cheatin' heart will tell on you.

Why? Because a chair falls to the floor.
Because a voice rises and breaks,
rises and breaks like a glass shattering,
a door slamming, skin opening again
to the old story of the day after
and after and glued things living
in the silence of pretending they aren't.
Because mending takes these small
precise steps, stitches one after another
on the jagged underside of hurt—
lives seamed smooth now and straight:
clocks only clocks, not instruments of countdown.
In this museum of innocent objects—photos,
yardstick, keys, telephone book, suitcase,
hairbrush, money—no one holds their breath
listens to the same stories, the same stories,

while pouring the brown liquid
like a fairytale witch pouring *just so* into glasses,
knowing each one could be the amber
that shifts the night's dark balance.

Because survival is finally just survival:
a child's hands holding the curtain closed
longer, better, letting no light out—or in.

Playing Percentages

The long medicinal hallways of childhood fear.
The stale paper rooms of catholic grade school.
Salted-in-the-shell peanuts at cigar smoke pool halls.
How indelible each lonely hour.

How we waited, paid with strawberry pop
to watch them break themselves,
one against another like stags in rut
or in a magazine loneliness we could not enter.

Each joy temporary like the rainbowed fall gardens.
Black and barefoot toes washed under a hose.
The earth taste of harvest—soon boiled away.
Winter rooms a brandy crowd of angry.

What would we call back of all that gone?
What price pay memory gods to level or sort?

The Way We Love Something Small

Pause before the mirrored gray
of thinning hair. Grant parole.

With grace, revisit days of small
wanting—glass jar on firefly
nights, moon a ripe song over water.

And something wakening.

Now the angle of face
lit by campfire, that laugh
ringing a bell inside us,
its echo a touch, re-naming.
Each soft space. Each sunrise.

How simple longing.　　A bliss.
A ceremony.
　　　　　　　　Without excess.
Its light, though tiny,

still spirals.

Grace Notes

Each skirt flounce hungers the toe of my tallest boots. My eyes eat collar points,
each pearl shirt button, the bolo snaking down his chest. Fiddle notes sweeten
September's chill air. Leaves—a bronze flame in the oak, a copper confetti
on the pavilion floor.

Deliberately I tip my head. Let eyelashes curtain longing.

Knees lift again like a smile. Feet shuffle—forward, back. His slim-legged jeans
glide and cross, glide and cross. Thumbs tuck in belt loops and steer.

Amnesia comes, but arms remember the spin out and under. The twirl takes me.

I am music, an angled bow, a banjo pluck.

Beneath the Berry Moon

Nii bas giizis, oh Night Sun,
what mischief have you made?
Ode'iminikewi-giizis—Oh heart moon,
when berries the size of your fingernail
bloom and ripen, fragrant and dangerous
as night under June summer sky. Oh globe
of perfect greed, midnight *giizis* who watches
how sweetly they entice and fill us. On tongues
their glib red holy satisfying as kisses.
But oh, Strawberry Moon, you also feed us hunger
for more days of copper sun and loon nights.
Under your tickling light lovers call like owls:
Who whoo? Oh you yoooou, only you!
When our strawberry hearts stretch in languid air,
the wayward fruit of your longing ours,
see how full moon eyes of sweethearts glimmer—
how fleeting, the jealous glow of summer.

An Old Story

A man wears northwoods plaid. He pedals everywhere. Once he had a crush on my mom. He never married.

The story lifts itself out of a place I understand.

They grew up, family. Running a little bit tame, a little bit wild. She bit into the bitterest plants and laughed. He followed, a shuffle step, a shadow.

Chapters two, three, and four. He came to town, stopped in for coffee. Fingered and fingered our thin playing cards for cribbage with my dad. Brought us whiskery deep-toned stories, awkward gifts.

In those years, I watch him watch her hands. She molds and shapes pie crusts, then knife-pricks the perfect tops. Makes a flower pattern of steam holes.

After. He mourned her in ways more public than the rest of us. Cancer walk-a-thon. Lighted candles.

I didn't look away.

Perhaps even now:

How the honey on the counter catches light.
How the early snow circles the dark mound.
Perhaps you do not understand   the alone we are

between the bees gold
                              and the fresh turned earth.

Here.
              Perhaps.
Even now.

              Alone.

Tonsorium

Remember the clandestine afternoon?

Your brother wielding a scissors. Random locks of hair on the floor
at your feet.   Hunting for a broom, a hat. And giggles.

> Jagged
>> just a game.

Today I watch the auburn strands hit the sink. Guilty again. But who is left
to scold? Repair as my mother did—her lips thinned to a cutting edge.

Mirror, Mirror. A tricky partner in this pandemic affair. Ah, perspective—
I turn my wrist this way, that.
>> Too often I miss . . .

> Cut emptiness.

As if my now gloved hands were secrets

my fingers dream names to fist,
keep close as folded blackbird wings.
Or to spread o p e n – like a shelter,
a tent of the temporary
red-songed as May mornings.

As if each coo and trill were a roll-call,
a sharpened alphabet of the absent.
The notes of names repeating,
repeating like days like solitary—
this hypnosis of imagined safety.

As if the globe of sun were a medicine.

As if rhyme gave us moorings.

As if soaping finger play were a classroom:
Here is the beehive,
Where are the bees?
Hiding inside where nobody sees!

As if distance were only a game.

As if my fingers were spring seedlings
swimming in the moist black of earth
surrounded by dark   aloneness
surrounded by stay stay, stay at home.

As if my hunger could spread a table.

As if planted and watered with distance,
these now untouchables would grow
handily, grow to be handy, handsome—
as if hands will grow welcome again.

As if leaf—the green reach of palm—were mine.

As if hands were a mantra of memory:
each hoe, each kettle handle and knife,
each keyboard, hairbrush, door knob turning,
each phone, button, dial, face—each touch
a familiar, this crave restless for coupling.

As if fingers on the heart planchette
of Ouija were a science.

As if pencil were a penicillin,
poetry a contagion of compassion.

As if flood of wetlands were an allegory for hope.
As if we were seeping close closer—nodistance.

Prayer in the Wake of Transience

How once your voice escaped on the wind.
How we climbed after, scoured the skies
where flapping hundreds, translucent
wings repeat a language called motion,
like the one backward glance caught
in the wake of all things leaving.

What we cannot name nor hold
in anxious pockets, in camera reality,
neither in hands nor tightly in mind—
our child's babble turning over, hour
by hour growing, to fill our hungry cells
with vibration—their stories, honeyed wisdom.

Yes, we will listen now in kitchens,
hold our breath beside cooling bread pans,
then whistle the practiced loon call
across dark surfaces of northern lakes.
A gesture, one half of unfinished business—
not anticipation, but the sure harvest still claimed.

Let us bless then the hollowed out sorrows
of flesh, bless what we neither wish
nor invite; perhaps the purple ache of shadows
will part, emptiness stand open like a portal.
Before this small fissure in darkness, make offerings
of your brokenness. Across the silence—send songs.

iv

The Way We Love Something Small

In the shadow of moons.
A battered canoe
on my back, the weight—

a hunger
calling like all aches for remedy,
for deeds   to carry me

across the endless
          unspoken.

Waters filled with lost dead
who also paddled   green island mornings
dipped their hands
          into frigid water.

Waking inhaled
  pine-scented   aloneness.

Here. Bird-joy lilting across lake fog—
a sweet keen.

Remembering you
          with the lust of moons.

If Scintilla is a Flowering Luminous as Night

Our blue hunger like the skin of midnight   waits.
Still gangly, growing in curve   like young trees
we lift bark eyes,   make of lips   a grass whistle
                                  a longing . . .

Again dark   is punctured: silver ~ green ~ neon
motion spills   sudden
Aurora   (all mouths agape).

How we drink   from fissures—
    elegant our hope   in streaks   glitter
        gold   when old souls dance—*niimi' idiwag*.

Sky gods make music with lights—
    waawaateg.   This spiral abundance
      like a fringed shawl.   Small moons,
crescents,   we love the large swallowing.

We too open
      like *bagone-giizhik*—hole in the sky.
How trace the ancestors' steps—
                this path   of souls
ephemeral   as motion,   as each song of northern lights.

Aanikoobijiganag—yes, call them   closer
here where worn memory   stretches   to dome the sky
here   where night swirls
                luminous   but fleeting.

The old one's feet like flint—each spark a fragment of fire,
ishkode   like tongues   burning time.

                   Effervescent   star story—
           crossing dimensions.

                            Our spirits.

Quiescence

i.

Soft pampas grass. We bed down like deer, rest after the dying. Spirits all walk toward horizon. Transform against the evening chrysalis of sky.

ii.

You feed me your dark-eyed loneliness, wisdom from Dr. Fauci, and sectors of tangerine small as my thumb. Scent the air. Everything is shrunken or overblown now.

I am undressing. Blue jeans, flannel. My polished toes naked in the damp tickling fronds. The bottom of my feet tender as story.

iii.

Soon we are turning to B&W. 100 years ago. Just before Betty White was born. Just before that other dying time. Those epidemic faces—framed like myth in our eyes.

Everybody sainted but us.

iv.

We tether ourselves, but things grow out of control. Network images on repeat— guns and knees, shattered windows, and black death. Plague upon plague.

v.

I keep seeing the picture of the elk, its antlers turned to tree. Bare black branches silhouetted against a stormy sky. In that tangle, a singing bird.

vi.

Let us stand now where the grass is tall, settle our legs there among the growing. Listen like all forlorn for the least crackle of air. Until the nocturnal bats hum our names.

Perhaps then we shall feel. Edges. Splintering. How soon a bough, a stem, a tributary? How soon we too shall antler like deer woman.

vii.

Yes, rise now—after the dying. Thick-necked and sturdy. Russet with hope—await the perch of bird.

The Way We Love Something Small

The translucent claws of newborn mice
this pearl cast of color,
the barely perceptible
like a ghosted threshold of being:
here   not here.
The single breath we hold
on the thinnest verge of sight:
not there   there.
A curve nearly naked,
an arc of almost,
a wisp of becoming,
a wand—
tiny enough to change me.

Another Poem in Which I Watch

Another morning ache
wakes me. Breath refusing
to come easy. I don't mean
this is a physical malady.
Perhaps not a malady.

This humanness wakes me.

An April in which I count
dark seeping out. Fragile
this time after dreaming,
before five, before going
to the window as I do.

When I do, I find you
grey against the eternal
mottle of winter leaves
this season we call *waitforrain*.

Find you not waiting
but finding. Tiny sprouts—
leaves or maybe only buds,
but green against the tired
carpet of what has fallen.

And you who do not pause
on the poetic side of longing.

This to be praised I think.

Here where I am still
at the window—still
watching, while oh florious
you are snapping the new
and eating all you can find!

Oh love, would it help to tell?

How your rough grey coat
is scarred—like me a patchwork
of what has not been kind
(and why I am awake too early
too worry and wanting the green
on my tired pandemic tongue).

I could keep the white secret
of your tail, fist this image
tight and open it again tomorrow
before five in the strangle of day.

Or I could follow your leap
into the dense hillside
of not yet, of soon—spend
that feast of flash, of bristle.

Like a flag they say, but no—
that won't do. Not today.
in aftermath of false patriots.
Here in the gloom grey broken
your scut a bloom, a bursting.

Where color is a small holy.

I watch each swift lift, each wave
a language of flare and fly.
Of sudden. And full on sublime.
Like the drama of roached heads
at a June pow-wow—yes, this arch
a sketch of dance. Fusion or trace.
Or enough—to start my breath again.

Oology

Finding shells in June,
pipped open and empty, scattered
like shed clothing across the forest floor.

Another abandoned spotted beginning. This half
of limitlessness.

Edges jagged. Blood-marked and fragile
membrane of egg. Sleeve. Sheath.
Shell.   Now sign of leaving.

Or arriving here at the notched rim
of transformation, where life gapes
wide—gapes new.

Imagine the softly feathered
bodies unwrapping wings still wet.

Or the curved flex of my own oval cage—
holding breath on one side, spilling it
invisible as longing on the other.

Waaban: ancient light enters

Crane curves of this woodland sky—

your floral wings a fissure:

Against beads of primal darkness
sky patterns pitch and slope into bloom.

Behind you ancient light enters.

Stitched here is first translucence:
sun turning the hose of your throat

to a vessel of fire.

Even now your body lengthens,
angled   like a sundial
against the cup of all reluctance:

our rock cold clan longing
weighted anchor of time.

Your voice a dawn—a torch of language.

Zhashagi

song flame of your tongue—
gives light.

Tracing, Kinship Lines

for Juane Quick-to-See Smith

Deep bellied world:
a prairie of saw blades and sweetgrass
skeleton fish who crossed realms
rice kernels and elk antlers
all watered by *manidoog*—tempestas
and *noodin* spirits, these sky relatives
who answer red willow-bark prayers.

i=ndigo lines
> *(how they feather brush and conjure*
> *animate geometry of angle, arc, of spiral;*
> *how color sacreds each relative—*
> *each broken*
> *a wing palette of translucence.)*

primordial genealogy
> *(makwa indodem, the climb of corn plants,*
> *bee buffalo raccoon branch lightning—*
> *each mothed starred and furred*
> *holy the hooved the leafed the four-winged kin.)*

How we story: water // bodies
crow and messenger shadows, *Memegwesiwag.*
Each feast, spirit plate, offering of *asemaa*
a follow—how lines of pencil smoke lift like music,
scent and conjure *mino-bimaadiziwin.*
transform into animaled eyes masks claws. Into crossings:
no lock, no chain of being—only this blue brush
                                        of likeness.

Nocturne at 2 a.m.

Imagine our paddling until a full-star sky,
my daughter freshly twenty-one,
the Milky Way—a sky of ancient enveloping us,
goblet of night alight with silver.

How to write swallowed, trace our vanish
into damp caress? Around us water stretches
calm in a blue dark forever. A perhaps
world. Vast dome where it rains stars—
where they float   twinkling on all sides,
singing us now,   both empty and full.

You must not envy what happens next:
sit close in the rhythm of a small canoe
purpled by night, we becoming water,
becoming wave—spirit already sated
when vowels of loon call open the night,
rise in a great hollowness, echo in tremolo.
There is water in the song—a nectar, a silk.

We put down our oars then (holy abandonment),
lay back in the newness of unwritten night—
world brimming with what remakes us.
Impossibly, as the loon's song diminishes
an answer comes. From across the lake,
waves of the haunting music—crescendo
and diminuendo. Full-throated, call and response.
I think the stars danced then. I think we did.

Dibiki-giizis: cameo in which heron fills moon

Of Poetry and the Making of Lines

How delicate—
                          dark
material of dream.
What we become
in space:

  An etch-
      ing.
  Stilled
  vector—
     two   dimensions
  of
holy.

A cut-out
      hunger.
Sweet shadow-filled
                          trace—
how we bargain
against
lurid possession.

Silhouette
our edges
in
     L
     E
     T
     T
     E
     R
     S
     .

A Love Poem to *Common* Arrowhead

I trace the length
            of your leaf blade
larger than my hungry hand
pointed like all deeply-held secrets.

I whisper names: arrowhead,
water plantain, duck potato—
badakidoon.

Your tuber body
            my buried history,
the old dream where we all grow
wholesome and laughing—*nibi* time.

Anishinaabeg water nations
feasting on the submerged—
ancient plants
            and their stories.

On Mapping

i. when a legend spells destiny in parchment

Across the dynamic landscape of history
they set markers. Flags, teak ranging rods—
coordinates scattered like musket balls,
each quivering X marks a pirate's treasure.

Here the chiseled arrow like talon prints,
the surveyor's disc—a bronze benchmark.
A platform for each eagle measure they take—
vision leveled and looking. But hungry.

ii. when ideas spiral spiral and return

Now too we chart the ancient—pace off
pathways to mounds, clay inlays,
carved bone, copper, and mica—
with each storied tribal pigment, resist.

Old voices flutter—thunderbird messengers,
birchbark scrolls, pictograph traces. This map
(lost cadence, motion of oldest endurance):
For ancestors, a traveling song.

Of Pith and Marrow

Leaving, you paddle with tickle of danger
a breeze on your cheeks. Let it take you.
Yes, study the obtuse angle of trees lining shore,
mark carefully your belated return—fool yourself;
evening's changing light will surely shutter that door.
Now taste how we hunger, lean in to fierce corners—
holy lodges named solitude, coals of forgotten fires.
Sprinkle them with the rough of cedar needles,
this scent map, memory marrow of oldest home.
Again follow: river otters, the flight of shipoke,
echoed call of loons—in the wake of a sweet bewitching.
Soon pulse of day quickens, shadows cannibal themselves;
so reach, inhabit fear like air in fluted stone, like belonging.
Here each sun lengthens copper on the water, copper
too, your exhaled breath, formed of thinnest shale.

The Way We Love Something Small

Inky leaf shadows on snow,
each animal track a hollow:
trace of bird feet, double oval of deer;
the glyphs we make—

the ones we follow.

Of Palimpsest & Vision

Against amber sky the antler of tree,
on mound of ledge rock an ochre pictograph—
thunder being or water bird, mythic
silhouettes alive like refracted realities.

Here dew on spider filament glistens—
orbs tensile with desire. Vines reach, twine
over stone, over hooves—everywhere layers.
Each silk trace an earth sutra, a thread of knowing.

Now clouds spiral in abundance, fall air fills
with thrum of wingbeats—with cycle.
This vibration ancient as sky's allegiance,
ancient as violet rivers carving granite.

Like amphibians in winter we, too, sink deep,
patient as sphagnum moss—wait for return.

Mazinigwaaso: Florets

When I embroider flowers, I inhale
remember again each petal-deep pocket,
each blossom like a tiny hand lifted.
Misko'o (red the dress of other murdered).

My fingers hunger. Stitches, calloused tips
an offering to florals and woodland spirits
who have curved our bodies in season—
centers a holy that opens damp with nectar.

Wanton our bloom; wanton our disappearance:
ikwewag, women wild and heedless as flora
in a world innocent of scythe and pesticide—
innocent of trampling oil nations who own.

Waabigwaniikaag, an abundance we make
of the broken—when burst becomes seed.

sub-imago (shedding names)

Where *zaaga'igan* ripples like corduroy,
checkered bodies bob on the wake,
fish-weed-iron scent and feet in silt—
glare on a crossing boat is news.

I am aging out of survey boxes.
We want off the Schoolcraft map
islands like dances we have saved,
my canoe paddle hungers in rhythm.

Manidoog have written on the rocks—
pictographs and water levels imprinted
old markers shimmer—alive on northern air.
Lake is a calendar like harvest.

We are lunar. When *ode'iminike-gizis* rises,
mayflies sprinkle water with translucence,
their tiny bodies feed *ogaawag*, feed us.
Still jagged, we offer song and gifts of *asemaa*—

all these tobacco ways we feast spirits.
No need to speak of treaty, scars—of healing.
We tell cribbage hands under this ancient—
star story-wolf howl-berry cloth of kinship.

Legacy

Antler earrings carved by gone hands,
birchbark baskets, ruby star quilt—
I could fill this page with left behind
with tattered—this legacy.

My house can hardly hold the loss,
my body.

Ancient one.

What then shall I leave you
of words?

ACKNOWLEDGMENTS

THE INHERENT irony in my work as a literary artist: I create in solitude in order to build community. The pandemic changed social dynamics for all of us, yet we need community more than ever. I express my inadequate thanks for the generosity of individuals and communities who have supported me or championed my work over the years, and who devised new ways to stay connected—even as the world sheltered in place. For space or time to write, monetary support, reading of drafts, performance and exhibit invitations, tech assistance, and innumerable other kindnesses, I say miigwech. To spirit advisors (in this world and others), zaaga'idiwin.

I am particularly indebted to In-Na-Poets (intrepid board—past and present, fellows, and DC faculty for Indigenous Nations Poets). I celebrate you here: Laura Tohe, Luci Tapahanso, Jennifer Foerster, Jake Skeets, Joy Harjo, Heid Erdrich, Elise Paschen, Denise Low, Leanne Howe, Craig Santos Perez, Cedar Sigo, Esther Belin, Deborah Miranda, Edgar Silex, Lee Francis IV, Janet McAdams, Michael Wilson, Margaret Noodin, Ashley Houghton, Arielle Taitano Lowe, Kenzie Allen, Manny Loley, Tacey Atsitty, Annie Wenstrup, Halee Kirkwood, Rena Priest, Max Early, Kinsale Drake, Kalilinoe Detwiler, Mary Leauna Christensen, Anthony Ceballos, Ha'áni Lucia Falo San Nicolas, Amber McCrary, Casandra López, Kristina Togafau, and Bodera Joe. A debt of gratitude as well to the Poetry Coalition, the Academy of American Poets, the Poetry Foundation, Storyknife Writers Retreat (my lovely cohort—Leticia Del Toro, Claudia Mauro, Maria Isabelle Carlos, Elena Passarello, Pik-Shuen Fung, Patrice Gopo; the staff—Erin Hollowell, Maura Brenin and Katie Emerick; and moose visitors), the Wisconsin Academy of Sciences, Arts, and Letters,

Native Writers' Circle of the Americas, past and present members of the Wisconsin Poet Laureate Commission (especially Nick Demske, Peggy Rozga, and Angie Trudell Vasquez), Woodland Pattern Book Center (especially Jenny Gropp, Laura Solomon, Mike Wendt, and Peter Burzynski), American Literature Association Taiwan (especially Hsinya Huang), Wisconsin Fellowship of Poets, Institute of American Indian Arts, Council of Wisconsin Writers, Aldo Leopold Center, the incredible staff at the Library of Congress (especially Rob Casper, John Fenn, and Barbara Bair), the Museum of Wisconsin Art, Playa, Wick Poetry (especially David Hassler), Poetry of Resilience (Danusha Laméris and James Crews), Split This Rock (especially Rasha Abdulhadi and Camisha Jones), Adrian Brinkerhoff Poetry Foundation, Tippet Rise Art Center, Alexandre Gallery, AICHO, Wisconsin Library Association, Walker's Point Center for the Arts, UW-Milwaukee and the Electa Quinney Institute, Patricia Rovzar Gallery and Gail Severn Galleries, Gathering Ground (Alessandra, Russell, Adrian, and now—Zebulon!), and Write-On, Door County. Heartfelt gratitude to Éditions des Lisières for *Résister en dansant / Ikwe-niimi: Dancing Resistance*, where some of these poems first appeared.

Finally, I express immense gratitude to the staff at the University of Arizona Press for their personal warmth and careful shepherding of *Ancient Light* through the publication process. Special thanks to Leigh McDonald for her lovely design work and to Amanda Krause for extraordinary sleight of hand and willingness to attend to the nuances of the poems as she guided every production detail. Most of all, miigwech to my editor, Elizabeth Wilder, for her deep reading, helpful insights on my work, and willingness to talk poetry because sometimes talking poetry is what we need to continue.

More individuals than I can count have graced me with their wisdom and friendship. Special missives of appreciation to Robert and Lenor Blaeser; pen-pal and sister in boldness, Joni Tevis; dream-maker Kathy Engel, Jen Benka, past students (read: teachers), and worker bees (better than applause bees!) Ryan Winn and Emma Knickelbine. The list goes on, but let me just add Willow who always reminds me to venture forth where there are scents, animals, plants, water in all shapes and sizes—worlds to discover which we will each chew in our way.

Most importantly, to Len, Amber, and Gavin, to my extended family, and to friends who have become family, I owe a debt of gratitude for patience, love, food, outdoor adventures, laugh fests, dreams, card games, music, and the little pieces of your soul you shared. You are here—in every word.

My thanks to the editors of the following publication venues where versions of these poems first appeared:

- "Poem on Disappearance," *Living Nations, Living Words: An Anthology of First Peoples Poetry*, and the "Living Nations, Living Words" audio project, Library of Congress
- "Dead Letter," *One Poem: A Protest Reading in Support of Black Lives.* Poetry Coalition digital program.
- "About Standing (in Kinship)," *Poetry.*
- "The Way We Love Something Small: The Translucent Poems of Newborn Mice," Poem-a-Day, Academy of American Poets.
- "The Where in My Belly," "Vote the Earth," a project of Wick Poetry.
- "Nocturne at 2 a.m.," "sub-imago (shedding names)," and "Taxonomy," *Prairie Schooner.*
- "Another Poem in Which I Watch" and "Dead Letter," *Cutthroat: A Journal of the Arts.*
- "Truce," "An Old Story," and "Found Recipe, Mikinaak Dibaajimowin," *Yellow Medicine Review: Women's Wisdom, Women's Strength.*
- "On the Dignity of Gestures" and "Rosetta Stone," *About Place Journal: Dignity as an Endangered Species in the 21st Century.*
- "Of Universal Suffrage," Project 19, New York Philharmonic.
- "A Water Poem for Remembering," Poem of the Week, Split This Rock, The Quarry.
- "Of Pith and Marrow," *Water Stone Review.*
- "How Love Balances on Each Precipice," *Midwest Review.*
- "The Way We Love Something Small: Vowel sounds from a land," Siwar Mayu, http://siwarmayu.com/balance-on-the-verge-of-vision-kimberly-m-blaeser/.
- "Alaskan poems I didn't write" and "The Way We Love Something Small: Pause before the mirrored gray," *Through This Door: Wisconsin in Poems.*
- "On Mapping," *Wisconsin People and Ideas: 150 Years.*
- "The Knife my Father Gave Me at Eight," *In Other Words: Poems by Wisconsin Poets in English and Chinese.*
- "Tonsorium," *Sheltering with Poems.*
- "*Gitigaanan*" and "A Love Poem to Common Arrowhead," *Claiming Space: A New Century of Visionary Women*, Wisconsin Museum of Art.
- "*Mashkiki*: This Medicine Earth," Wisconsin Public Television.
- "Plead the Blood" and "When We Have Lost Enough," *The Poets' Republic.*
- "Oology," *Poetry Hall: Chinese and English Bilingual Journal.*
- "As if my now gloved hands were secrets," *Gatherings*, Patricia Rovzar Gallery and Gail Severn Gallery.
- "Tracing, Kinship Lines," *About Place Journal: Navigations: A Place for Peace » Gratitude: Solace, Sacredness.*
- "Here We Begin With Gesture," "*Mazingwaaso*: Florets," and "*Binesiwag*," *Under a Warm Green Linden.*
- "dream of birch-winged eagles" and "Sandhill sky," *Wildlife Stewardship on Tribal Lands.*

- "English Lessons," *Echoes: An Anthology of Native Women Writing Toward the Future.*
- "A Catalogue of Migration" and "Of Palimpsest and Vision," *Alexandre Gallery.*
- "see us sacred ≠ Xtracted," *No More Stolen Sisters,* Walker's Point Center for the Arts.
- "Understory," Wausau Poetry Walk.
- "Songs Like Bread: Wiikwandiwin," *How We Reclaim & Commemorate: An Anthology of Multilingual Poetry and Poetics.*
- "*Indian Baby in Front of an Indian Bldg,*" *Yellow Medicine Review.*
- "Quiescence" and "Beneath the Berry Moon," *Studies in American Indian Literatures.*
- "*Gitigaanan*" and "In the pause before you speak," *FIVES: a companion to Denver Quarterly* and *Westerly Online.*

ABOUT THE AUTHOR

Kimberly Blaeser, former Wisconsin Poet Laureate and founding director of In-Na-Po, Indigenous Nations Poets, is a writer, photographer, and scholar. Her five previous poetry collections include *Copper Yearning, Apprenticed to Justice,* and *Résister en dansant/Ikwe-niimi: Dancing Resistance.* Blaeser, a citizen of White Earth Nation, is the recipient of a Lifetime Achievement Award from Native Writers' Circle of the Americas. She is an Anishinaabe activist and environmentalist, a Professor Emerita at UW–Milwaukee, an Institute of American Indian Arts MFA faculty member, and the 2024 Mackey Chair in Creative Writing at Beloit College.